Kiss the Bear!

(And Other Outrageous Things God Asked Me to Do)

by
Rick Barker

PublishAmerica
Baltimore

First printing

At the specific preference of the author, PublishAmerica allowed this work to remain exactly as the author intended, verbatim, without editorial input.

ISBN: 1-4241-2449-2
PUBLISHED BY PUBLISHAMERICA, LLLP
www.publishamerica.com
Baltimore

Printed in the United States of America

Dedication

To my wife, Marci, and my children, Dustin and Denai, who have enriched my life beyond my imagination.

Acknowledgments

I am thankful to God for my wife, Marci, who encourages me along life's journey, who laughs at my jokes, and who sticks with me through all of life's challenges.

I thank God for my children, Dustin and Denai, who have provided me with so many stories and illustrations over the years.

I thank God for my brother and sisters, Arlene, Karen, Gale, Rod, and my mom and dad, Lloyd and Evelyn Barker. I love my family.

I am also grateful to God for all the people at Cariboo Christian Life Fellowship, upon whom I get to bestow my humor, my wisdom, my style of preaching and leadership—and to know you still like me...thank you for your love and patience!

Contents

Chapter 1
The Revelation

The Son of Man came to seek and save that which was lost.
—Jesus of Nazareth, Luke 19:10

So there I was, a 'noble and respected' pastor of a small community in the Interior of British Columbia, about to enter into the twilight zone of a local pub—about to go where "no man has gone before" to do what I was about to do.

With one more breath of prayer, I pushed open the saloon-style doors and stepped into the foreign world of dimly lit, smoke-filled noise. I squinted to adjust my eyes to my surroundings; heads turned to see who it was that entered their domain, friend or foe, and little did I know that my world was about to be changed forever.

What in the world was I doing, you ask?

Well, let me take you back a couple of months prior to venturing out into the neighborhood tavern. Life for me was generally the same as for most pastors—meeting with people, assisting them in their day to day stuff, shepherding them through the speed-bumps and potholes of life, preaching and preparing, praying and leading the family of God, looking at times to that distant question of "How will I reach this community for Christ?" but always coming up a bit short because of all the things that typically fill up a pastor's most precious book besides his Bible—his coveted day-timer.

Then one night, God spoke to me in a dream.

Now, God has spoken to me many times through dreams, downloading revelation, new ideas, scripture and direction. In fact, my whole step into a life of "full-time" ministry was initiated by the Lord through a dream. My wife, Marci, had told me that very night that she felt God would speak to me in a dream, but as a typical husband, I thought... "Well, whatever..." But He did, and it launched us into ministry, and into an adventuresome journey that I wouldn't trade away for a million bucks. And, while I know some people have trouble with the whole dream thing, I have searched the scriptures and found that there is a huge amount of biblical precedent for God speaking in dreams, both in the Old and the New Testament.

Immediately I think of Joseph and his dreams found in Genesis 37; I think of David writing in Psalm 127 how the Lord "gives to His beloved in their sleep," how Daniel called God, "the Giver of dreams and the Interpreter of dreams" (Daniel 5:12), how Daniel himself had dreamt many dreams that stirred his heart. I think of how Joel prophesied (2:28) that old men will dream dreams, and young men see visions in the last days, and how many dreams played a part in the birth of our Lord Jesus—with Joseph, both in the birth, marriage to Mary, and with the escape to Egypt, and subsequent return to Israel, plus with the Magi, or wise men as well, warning them not to return to Herod but to go home instead by another route.

In addition, Peter had dreams from God, and experienced night and day visions, as did John and Paul (the man from Macedonia, plus the Lord speaking to him in Corinth). The list goes on. Anyway, all that to say, I believe we serve the God who speaks today, as Job 33:14 affirms: "God does speak, now one way, now another, though men may not perceive it."

Back to the story at hand—God spoke to me in a dream.

I dreamt that I was walking along a forest road with my earthly father, who went to be with the Lord in 1989 (my dad was set free from alcoholism dramatically by God and was always quick to tell the story after that). In my dream I turned to my right and was surprised to see a young boy of around 12 years old with long brown hair out in the wilderness. There was deep gully on the side of the road where I stood, and a river below; the boy was on the other side of the river walking out from a thicket, leading a donkey that was pulling a cart. He was walking right toward the river and I was afraid for him, although he showed no signs of being uncomfortable. I lost sight of him so I went closer to the edge of the road, to the beginning of the gully to look over to see if I could spot him. There he was walking right into the river! And, I was surprised to see the donkey already in the river—doing the backstroke! It was like a cartoon, as only a donkey could do a backstroke, but I didn't laugh in my dream; it seemed to be no big deal to me at the time. But I was worried about the boy.

I turned around to talk to my father and suddenly this boy was in my face. I mean, literally, he was about 12 inches away from my face, now a little larger than a boy and he was peering into my eyes with intensity that blazed like fire. I realized as I looked into his eyes that this was no ordinary boy. It was in fact, Jesus, my Lord, and my Savior and He was looking intently into my very being. He spoke and the sound of the voice was all that I could hear or focus on. These are the words He said:

"People look for me in many different ways. But I search for people...in bars, and at parties."

Then, not taking His eyes from mine, He gave a coy, almost mischievous smile as if he was about to surprise me, and surprise me He did! He jumped right into me! I mean, He literally leapt into my very chest, inside of my spirit and I awoke from the dream with a start. I sat there awake in the middle of the night, wondering what this meant, and I questioned the Lord on it before falling asleep again.

The next morning, my wife Marci and I were heading out of town for a conference and we were discussing the dream. I told her I felt that it was a commission from God. In the dream, Jesus told me He searches for people—that is He's active, not passive. He is searching. His heart really is for the lost, as Matthew 19:10 declares, "The Son of Man came to seek and save that which was lost."

The donkey and the cart represented the harvest that is ripe. Jesus being represented as a boy seemed to emphasize childlike faith and joy in the harvest. My earthly father being there reinforced evangelism. Jesus is searching, searching…and then He jumps right inside of me. Jesus inside of me, the Hope of Glory, is searching and using my eyes, my hands, my feet, actively looking for the lost and then reaping the harvest. Where? *In bars and in parties.* Oh my goodness! Does that mean…do I have to…yes! That was what that coy smile was all about. That would mean I would have to climb out of my comfort zone and go where the Holy Spirit wanted to go, speak to whom He wanted me to speak, go into the local bar for a starter, and see what He had in mind. The timing had to be right, the prayer-cover, the motivation—everything had to revolve around being obedient to the voice of the Holy Spirit saying "Now, now is the time." As my dad used to say: "When I say jump, you say 'how high?'"

So, there I was. It was a Friday night; I was on a prayer walk—believe me I was praying! "Lord, You said You search for people; You are inside of me by Your Holy Spirit. You are directing me to go into the bar tonight; I am simply following Your lead. I have no idea what will take place. Lead on, Lord Jesus."

I pushed opened the doors.

Chapter 2
The Harvest

Look up for the harvest is plentiful but the workers are few. Ask the Lord of the harvest therefore to send out workers into His harvest field.—Jesus of Nazareth, Matthew 9:37

Now, I have to admit I am a fairly well known person in our small town of 2000 people, partly because I used to be a journalist at the local paper for five years, partly because I am a public entertainer with ventriloquism, and then there's the pastor thing, which means occasionally leading public funeral services and marriages. And, did I mention that I've lived here for over 30 years? Needless to say people did double-takes as I walked into that dark cavern of fellowship.

Immediately, I was hit by the smell of beer, which brought flooding back a rash of memories of my own dip into alcohol and drug abuse in my young adult years, but those memories were quickly pushed to the side when I scanned the room and noted that about nine backslidden Christians were in there. My heart went out to those prodigals, as I am sure the Lord's does as well. I walked over toward "the bar" of the bar, trying to look as if I knew what I was doing—you know, kind of John Wayne-like. I imagined that this must be what it's like for someone brand new going into a foreign place like a church.

"Who do I look at? What do I do? Who do I smile at? Am I supposed to kneel? What is this? A bulletin...oh, am I supposed to do something with it?"

The waitress, a backslidden Christian herself, came up to me with a smile. She knew me and asked boldly, "What are *you* doing here?"

I smiled. It was one of those times when just the right line was there on the tip of my tongue.

"I heard the fishin' was good."

She laughed and asked what I wanted to drink. I shouted at her (you have to shout to be heard). "Coke!" and she ambled away. She quickly came back and told me it was on the house. That was nice, I thought.

Well with Coke in hand, I slowly turned around and faced the crowd. I felt like it was slow motion as I was scanning the audience, thinking, praying, "Who are you searching for, Lord?"

My eyes locked with a young man whom I had met just the day before at the local high school. He was a journalist, actually doing the job that I used to do a number of years ago. His name was David and he motioned for me to come and sit. He looked like a lost puppy, all by himself in the midst of a crowd. He was in his twenties, had long curly hair and a nice disposition. He was alone so I thought, "Here goes" and I plunged in.

Parenthetically, I should note that when you are in this mode of evangelism, you kind of get into a zone where you simply are doing things, saying things that sometimes even surprise yourself, but if you abide in that place, fixed on the Lord, good things happen.

As I said, he indicated for me to sit down, which helped my comfort zone a little. Others, who knew me, walked by and said things similar to what the waitress had said such as "what are *you* doing here?"

I looked at David. He looked at me. And, then he said this...and remember the context of why I am here, what I am doing, first time to the bar in probably 22 years. Get this…he says, "Man, sometimes I do not know why the @#%& I am here!"

My response came out quicker than I expected it.

"I know why!" I shouted back at him. He looked at me with a quizzical look. I reintroduced myself and then, looking around the room, yelled over the crowd "My father used to live here in this bar! He was the town drunk, until something happened that really changed his life!"

There it goes. That was the casting of the line, or the tossing of the net. Remember Jesus talking about the kingdom of heaven being like a net that is tossed into the lake and becomes full of fish of all kinds? Ever feel the tug or nibble of a fish at the end of a line?

He bit.

"So, what happened to him, some sort of *Touched By An Angel* thing?" he asked, referring to a primetime television show that depicts angels interacting with humans in dramatic fashion.

"Bigger," I said.

About 10 seconds of time went by, but it seemed like at least 30 as I awkwardly sipped my Coke…

"Well, if you don't mind me asking, can you tell me the story?" he pressed. Inside, I thought, "okay, tuck your toes in, because here I come!"

And so I yelled the testimony of my father, Lloyd Barker, who had moved to our little town of 100 Mile House, B.C. in 1969-70 from the streets of Vancouver to sober up after some 30 years of alcoholism. He was skid row material, a derelict, drinking anything and everything. Vanilla extract was not below his dignity he used to say.

Sobering up didn't work. He became our town drunk—you know, the guy you see stumbling in a ditch late at night, or sitting on a curb during the day, dirty, gaunt and unshaven…that was my dad. I was about 10 or 11 at the time. He spent most of his time in the very bar that we were now sitting in, slept in a cabin up the highway a few kilometers.

One night he stumbled into the back of a local church, a church not known for having anything out of the ordinary ever happen, until that particular weekend that is.

There was a traveling evangelist in town, and he was holding some meetings at this little church. My dad, drunk as a…(Do skunks really get drunk?) town drunk can be, found his way into a back pew and fell asleep during the sermon. He got up and left about three-quarters of the way through the service, and drove his old car to the cabin where his friends were partying.

The story goes that the evangelist asked some of the church elders who that man was. They told him, "Oh that's Lloyd Barker," and basically indicated he was a lost cause.

"That man needs to be set free!" the evangelist exclaimed to them, and asked them to find him and bring him in for prayer.

It was early the following morning that they drove their van into the driveway where my father was staying. They didn't know that during the previous night, he had tried to commit suicide but the Lord had mercifully prevented it. He had parked his Chevy by the side of the highway, lifted the hood and stood in front of the car. He was simply waiting for a semi-truck to come by and he would push himself out into the path of it. He said he had totally given up on life, had failed his wife and five kids, had failed his God (given his life to Christ at age 11), failed everything—the devil was out to destroy this man and was nearly successful.

Despite this highway being the main corridor between Vancouver and the north, which has about 10 eighteen-wheeler trucks a minute passing through, not a single truck came by for over 20 minutes. Dad said he felt like even more of a failure because he couldn't even succeed at taking his own life. He was completely in despair. Later, he would say that God held up the traffic that night, just for him.

He recalled the men driving up to the cabin. "They looked like giants," he said. And they told him, "You're coming with us, Lloyd." He didn't argue but was helped into the van. He said he was so weak, not having eaten for days.

Back at the church, they took my dad into a small room where this evangelist simply asked him his name.

"I'm Satan," dad said in a voice that wasn't his own.

"Well, whoever you are," the evangelist commanded, "you come out of him right now in the name of Jesus!'And, to the amazement of the wide-eyed deacons watching this drama unfold, Dad shrieked and convulsed, his wine-stained shirt literally ripping in shreds off his back, top to bottom, as he was set free by the resurrection power of Jesus Christ, the risen and strong Son of God!

Dad was literally set free! He never, ever touched a drink again, nor even craved one for the rest of his earthly life, almost 20 years of freedom. He was also healed of angina, where he needed a triple bypass one day, and the next day, he didn't. Needless to say, he was a guy who loved to tell his story. His favorite song was the old hymn *He Touched Me*.

So like I said, there I was, in the bar, telling the story now to David as I told it above, and David's eyes were becoming quite large.

Dad's story naturally leads into my own testimony of drug and alcohol abuse, and how God rescued me out of that, put my life back on solid ground, and...

"Oh," I said, "I forgot to tell you what I do now. I'm the pastor at Cariboo Christian Life Fellowship (CCLF) here in town."

Well, he gathered up his chin from the floor and looked at me for a bit. He then asked the obvious question that others had been asking all night.

"So what are *you* doing here?"

"Well, I believe God speaks today, though people don't always hear Him. Sometimes He speaks to me through dreams."

I then told him my dream about the Lord searching for people in bars and parties.

"That is why I am here. God is searching for you."

Believe it or not, he said, "I think He is." He then told me how he was raised as an agnostic-near-atheist but the last few months he has been thinking more about God. In fact, he had prayed to God for the first time on his trip from Toronto to 100 Mile House in order to get through a snowstorm, and God had answered that prayer. He then had met a waitress in town who gave him a Bible, which he had begun to read.

He had some questions about some of the things he was reading.

I don't know about you, but sometimes I listen to people and carry on another conversation in my head at the same time. This time I was listening to him ask me questions and at the same time, marveling at how the Lord had set this up. I was praising the Lord for the perfect timing in all of this and how He led me here, this night, at this particular bar, to this particular table, to speak to this particular young man. Wow!

I answered his questions. He drove me home. I asked if I could pray with him, and he said he would like that, and so our relationship began.

The next week I was prayer-walking again, and asking the Lord about being led by His Spirit, and for some examples of when I have done that. The Lord said to me clearly, "remember the dream and the bar."

"Oh yes, I can't forget David," I was thinking. "That was pretty cool." My thoughts then went to David and I wondered if he might be interested in coming to a Christian men's conference with my son, Dustin, and I. Dustin was near his age, and it would seem more appropriate…I was thinking about this, then arguing with myself (ever do that?) that David was a journalist and would probably be very busy and he might be an atheist, and…I was going over excuses when suddenly I realized I had just walked past the man outside a local store!

"Hey Rick!"

"David!" I said.

"Hey, I was just thinking about you," he said.

Inside I was marveling again at the Lord's timing. "Really! I was just thinking about you."

"Oh? What about?" That was his investigative journalism training coming out no doubt.

So I just bluntly asked him, "Well…I was wondering if…you might want to come to a Christian men's conference—with Dustin and I…"

"Sure," he said.

It was at that men's conference that a speaker, a former NHL hockey player, gave his testimony of how he came to know Jesus, and the invitation to accept Christ as Savior and Lord. I watched as David mouthed the prayer in the stands and looked very sincere doing it. I kept thinking that this was all too easy; it all fell together, and there was no strain at all!

I asked him several times that weekend, "So are you in, or…?" He assured me that he was definitely in, and in fact, not two weeks later, he himself cast some demons out of a man! He was as in as in could be! He was and is so studious in the Bible that it amazes me. He lapped up the scripture, testifies all the time to everyone he can, and lives it out, never wanting to turn to the left or right. Oh,—and that waitress that gave him the Bible—she is now his wife. David and Megan are serving the Lord with all their might together in another community some three hours away.

You know what, the truth is, it was easy. It was all the Lord. He was searching. He was leading. He knew David before I did. He led me that night to the bar where David was; He led me to that particular table, to that particular young man that He had already been working on. David had already been on a journey, was already asking the questions; the Holy Spirit had already been drawing him, and I simply stepped into the Lord's timing, and picked a very ripe apple off the tree. It really was amazing.

I think we can learn some things from this. The harvest is indeed ripe. Jesus also said "My Father is always at work," and we can join Him in that work. He speaks today; we need to listen. He said His sheep know His voice. We need to pray and listen. We need to act; we need to dare to take risks, getting out of our comfort zones, off the sidelines and into the game. Whether it is sowing seed, watering, cultivating, or reaping, we can have joy doing it as we participate in the Father's rescue mission, the greatest mission of them all—to seek and save that which was lost. Let's look for those divine interruptions in our day, and always be alert for our opportunity to make the most of every opportunity! This is not something that only pastors can do, or the paid professionals. This is for all who name Jesus as Lord. He invites us to participate with Him in the greatest rescue mission ever launched.

And, I guess that begs the question, how do I know this is really God speaking to me?

Chapter 3
A Funny Thing Happened to Me on the Way to a Coffee…

My sheep know my voice.—Jesus, John 10:16

Who would have thought that God cared about my little Ford Tempo?

But you know what? God does care about the things you care about. I cared about my car, even if it was clunker at the time.

I was in youth ministry back then, and was in the city of Kamloops at a youth convention. I was parked at a local fast food joint, waiting for my teens to get their food and come out.

I was happy. I had everything I needed, namely my burger, my fries and my shake.

Then out of the blue, comes the thought: "I should park over there," looking at an empty parking stall across the lot. Then that old argument began. *"Why would I want to park over there? Why can't I just stay here; there's no reason to go moving the car now. The teens won't be able to find me…I think that's just stupid…"*

That's when I saw it.

I glanced in my rear view mirror and noticed a truck backing out of a stall behind me. I realized that the driver didn't see my car; he was going to back right into me! I must do something! I put my burger on the dash, spilled my milkshake and "meeped my little horn. Too late.

FHUMP! The sound of scraping metal sent a shiver up my spine. I steadied my milkshake but cringed at the hit as the driver turned around in disbelief; his bumper drove right into my trunk, denting it up and leaving a nice permanent reminder of the scriptures that say "he who has an ear, let him hear."

After the dust had settled, I remember my little argument I had had with my mind, will and emotions (soul) about moving the car.

Now wait just a minute! Was that God who suggested I move my car? Did He care about my little Tempo? Could it be? Could God be speaking to me about things like that?

The obvious answer to that question is: You bet!

I am reminded of the scripture I quoted earlier from the Book of Job, "God does speak, now one way, now another, though men may not perceive it." The trick is in the perceiving it. He who has an ear, let him hear. Does that mean, even those with ears, might not hear? Yup.

Right after that car incident, I decided to really try to pay attention to the Lord interrupting my thoughts and speaking to me on a daily basis. I really wanted to learn to listen, without going off the deep end, or becoming parked in section whacko, flakes-ville, psycho-world or the land of make believe.

Two days later, I was back in my hometown, had dropped off my son, Dustin and my daughter, Denai, at school, and was going to the corner store to pick up a coffee before heading to the office.

I noticed a little old lady out near her car at the gas pumps. I didn't take too much notice but the thought struck me to ask her if she needed any help because she looked a little bit perplexed. But I didn't because I thought that would be a bit rude and presumptuous of me (arguing again), and besides why would she be out there at the gas pump if she didn't know what to do. So I decided to mind my own business, went in, got my coffee, came out and found she was still there standing and staring at the pumps.

Now I couldn't resist. Why should I mind my own business when I should be about my Father's business?

"Do you need help?" I asked.

She nodded yes, and so I put my coffee on the roof of my car and went over.

You know what she said? Of course you don't. I'll tell you.

"My husband just died," she said. "He never taught me how to use one of these things." She started to cry and I realized that again, wow, this was a kingdom moment and I had almost missed it.

So I taught her how to use the self-serve pump, told her I was a pastor, and asked her if I could pray. It was a great time of ministry—which would not have happened, had I listened to the stupid argument. You have to step out, and you have to take risks. You have to dare. Why not? What's the worse thing that could happen? That's what I always ask now, and usually my answer is 'Well, they may kill me, but then I will be in heaven, so it's all good."

Later that same week at that same corner store, I went in to get my coffee before going to the office. The thought came in to my head, "I should pick up a Tribune this morning." Now you have to understand that I almost never read the Tribune; it is not our local paper; it is from another small community and for the most part, I could care less about what the Tribune has to say. When I was a journalist, it was our rival paper, so I had a bit of a bias about the whole thing. But today, I get this thought about picking it up. I looked at it. I even touched it. Then the clerk asked, "Will that be all?"

"Yup," I said and walked out with just my coffee.

I arrived at the office as usual and just as I was coming in, the phone rang. I picked it up with a hearty "G'd morning, CCLF, Pastor Rick here…" There was an older lady on the other end, who was crying because she was grieving the loss of her grandchild. You know what she asked me? DO YOU KNOW WHAT SHE ASKED ME?!

"Have you seen the paper this morning?"

I cringed inside as I asked her, "Which paper?" And yup, you know it, it was the Tribune. You see, on the cover of the Tribune was a picture of her grand-daughter who had just recently died. Now, had I picked up the Tribune, and read that first story, I would not have had to put this loving grandmother through the story all over again. I could have said, "Yes, I know all about it," and just minister to her need. But no, that time, I didn't listen to the still, small voice; I listened to my loud, overbearing argument that is anchored in pride—me, me, me. I repented before the Lord for this one and for all the other times when I fail to listen. You might think that this was a small, trivial thing. But it wasn't to that grandmother. And, the Lord cares about what people care about deep inside. He longs to have compassion on people, delighting over them with singing, wanting to quiet them with His love (Zephaniah 3:17). Oh no, it may be a small thing in our eyes, but God sees with a different perspective. Give me another opportunity Lord, just to hear Your voice, and obey.

And, He has given me more opportunities, some I have failed at, and some I have obeyed in. The times of obedience have always resulted in blessing, even if it wasn't obvious that another person was ministered to. I was blessed in my obedience, for sometimes I know He asks us to do things, simply to see if we will obey.

Like the time I was in Vancouver and I had been to a friend's church. The pastor had preached about always being ready, in season and out, to simply tell your story. At the end of the service, he brought us into a place of quiet, and he said, "Let God bring to your mind a name of someone. Perhaps you are to tell this person your story."

The name, David, came to mind. Now at that time, all the Davids I knew were Christians, so I sort of dismissed the thought, although it did cross my mind that maybe I would meet a David. So I prayed, "Lord if you want me to speak to a David, send me a David."

Well, a lot of funny things happen to me on the way to a coffee.

I pulled into a corner store, to grab a coffee (okay, okay, I know that it's getting obvious) and I was in line at the counter when my heart began to pound! It wasn't the caffeine. The clerk had a nametag on...and yes, printed on the nametag in letters that appeared to be three-dimensional as they leapt out and enlarged before my eyes, was: *David*.

He was a dark young man, probably of African descent and looked to be around 18 years old. I wondered "Gee, I wonder if he knows Swahili."

Now I realize that that is a silly thing to wonder, because I don't wonder that every time I run into a black person. This time, though, the thought struck me. You see, I know a little Swahili because a wonderful brother in the Lord, who was from Ethiopia, taught me some common words in Swahili, telling me that "One day you will need it."

As I moved closer to it being my turn at the counter, I noticed that the clerk, David, had a bracelet on and on the bracelet were some strange words.

"Hi," he said. "Will that be all?"

"What does your bracelet mean?"

"Oh," he said. "That's my name...in Swahili."

Inside, my heart is going BA—BAM! I again marvel at how the Lord does this, if we will simply let Him!

"Jumbo Endugo! Habadi Yacko?"—meaning hi brother, how are you?

Well, this dude's eyes almost popped out of his head as he looked at this white boy who was speaking his native language! Unbelievable! You know the Lord struck up a conversation there that was awesome. I had told him that I didn't think our meeting was an accident, but that God brought us together for some reason. In a matter of minutes, he literally unloaded to me all about his life, his struggles, and about his mother who was very ill, and in need of physical healing. I couldn't believe how open he was to receive ministry in the name of the Lord. And, all I came in there for was a coffee.

Now, I would love to say *"And then, David knelt down right there in the middle of the store and gave his life to Jesus,"* but that didn't happen. In fact, I never saw him again after that, but you know what, the story is not over. This David is just like that other David, whom I met in the bar, on a separate journey, to the Father of Lights. An old saying goes "The providence of God will always lead you to the God of providence." So I believe one day, I will see David again, and he will know the Lord, and may even testify about how one day as an 18-year-old clerk, there was this guy who came in and told him about Jesus.

So, back to that question, "Well, how do you know? How do you know whether it's God or just you?"

I guess in reality, you don't know right off. The more you step out, though, the more you begin to recognize the voice of the Holy Spirit. Jesus said the Holy Spirit would lead you, would speak to you, and would show you of things to come. He is your personal tutor and He will never, ever tell you to do something that goes against the written revelation of God's Holy Word, the Bible. In addition, He will always magnify the Son of God, Jesus Christ. That's His job, and He does it very well.

People ask, "But does He speak in the first person, or second person?"

Hey, He's God. He can do both. For me, He often speaks in the first person, meaning I will get a thought that is like: "I should do this, or I should do that; I should pick up that hitch-hiker; I should clean the sink, do the dishes…" Now I can hear some of you guys out there going "Wait a minute, don't get carried away!"

But I say, "Oh yes, do get carried away!" Listen to the Lord help you become a better husband, a kinder, gentler person, a godly man, a man of integrity. If God is whispering in your ear to clean the sink after you shave, you can respond by doing it, and thanking God that He is teaching you to be a better husband. It really is that simple.

As I said earlier, I have had many opportunities where I have missed the boat and missed the opportunity to step out of the boat. I see it in hindsight, and realize "Oops, that was God." But the more we obey God, the more we experience Him and the more we experience Him, the more we love Him, and the more we love Him, the more we will want to obey Him, and the more we obey Him, the more we will experience Him, and the more we experience Him, the more we love Him, and the…you get the picture.

Chapter 4
Kiss the Bear

Consider it pure joy my brethren when you fall into various trials, knowing that the testing of your faith produces patience.—James 1:2-3

Ever been chased by an overbearing, growling old grizzly bear? I have.

But I thank God that it was only in my dreams! In actual reality I really was chased by a black bear, but that's another story…

Pastoral ministry, as you know, has its ups and downs. Sometimes, a pastor is so totally amazed at the graciousness of the people he is called to serve, and at other times…well, other times remind me of 93-year-old pastor who stood up at a pastor's conference and said in an cranky old voice, "After 50 years in ministry, I have learned one thing—sheep bite!"

That's a BLT of ministry. A pastor buddy of mine named Pat, who has walked with me through tremendous waters under many bridges, coined that term and we laugh out loud when we talk about our BLTs (bottom line theology).

"Sometimes life sucks, but God is good," he'd say. That's a BLT. We have many more. One time he added one on to the "sheep bite" statement. He said "Yup, and sometimes sheep-bite can be fatal, which is why the Lord gives shepherds those staffs—not to scare wolves but to bat the sheep!" Perhaps you have to be a pastor to laugh at that but I think you understand.

Just before a period of time in my life that seemed to be full of sheep bites, goat butts and donkey kicks, not to mention a few of those wolves, I had a series of three dreams involving the exact same characters, in particular, two massive grizzly bears.

The first dream, I thought was just an interesting dream about two bears, one that was off doing its own thing, feeding on some bugs under a stump, and this other bear, which I knew was a big ol' male that swung its head toward me and started running right at me.

When it started running, I started running. I ran to my car, which of course, was locked. You can picture the scene, fumbling with my keys, bear getting closer, me looking over my shoulder, bear getting closer, fumbling, closer. I finally get the door open, jump in and slam the door shut just as the bear KABASHES my car by slamming into the side of it. I lay a strip of rubber as I peel away in my car, noticing that out of my trunk, a duffel bag flew open and a bunch of baggage was strewn all over the road. The last thing I recall of that dream was the bear pawing at my baggage.

I awoke from that, noting it, jotting it down in my journal but not really paying too much attention to it.

Until two nights later, when I had another dream. Same sort of scene unfolded—two bears, one eating away, the other picking up my scent, swinging its head about, then coming after me from across a field.

I began to pay attention, feeling that these dreams may be from the Lord, that He was inviting me into a time of seeking Him for the answer to the riddle of the dreams. What did these two bears mean? Why was one chasing me and the other not? What was going on?

Then, I had the third dream.

I remember it so vividly. I was out in the woods in a ramshackle little cabin, looking out what was once a window but now was just a bit of a hole in the wall. And, there they were.

Two bears, same grizzlies, one eating away like nothing was the matter, and the other sniffing the air. It was as if it knew the exact moment that I had noticed it. It lifted its massive head, swung it in my direction and started coming!

I pulled away from the window and looked around the cabin. There was nothing here to use as a weapon! It wasn't long before I could hear the bear right outside the door. I moved toward the window as it smashed its way through the door and came barreling into the one-room cabin! I jumped out the window and scrambled. Looking behind me as I tried to get up from the ground as quickly as possible, I noticed the bear was coming out the window, pearly white teeth snapping, fiercely growling. So I timed my escape and as soon as it came out the window, I went back in through the door! We did this a few times like in a cartoon, out the window, in the door, out the window, in the door. Then I just took off and started running through the woods. But that obsessive bear kept charging. It was serious.

I was panicking at this point because all around me were these wispy little aspen trees, nothing to climb at all. Have you ever tried running in your dreams only to find you're just going in slow motion, or you just can't…seem….to…move? It was like that.

I stopped and turned around to face the bear. I stood behind a little aspen tree about three inches in diameter, as if this would offer some protection. The bear kept coming, head moving up and down with each stride, saliva spraying from its mouth, its jowls going in and out like in slow motion. I could even smell its breath, as it got closer.

In desperation and fear, I yelled out to heaven "GOD, WHAT DO I DO!!?"

Believe it or not a voice came from heaven, which I knew to be God. It was solid, deep, very calm voice that could only be God!

"Kiss the bear."

"WHAT!?"

Again it came. *"Kiss the bear."*

So…yeah, I kissed the bear. I grabbed its face by its jowls and plunked a big ol' smack right on its snout.

The bear reared back with a stunned look on its face, and gave out a surprised, woofy, deep kind-of-grunt that only a grizzly bear could do. It sort of sounded like a cartoon character going "huhhhhhhhh?"

And then it dropped to the ground in defeat, and literally disintegrated, and then I awoke.

Actually, I awoke with laughter. I was laughing and asking God what in the world does all this mean?

Well, I asked a lot of people their thoughts about the dream; I got books about grizzly bears and what they are like; I scanned our dream books that suggested the bears represented the enemy, etc. etc. but I did not feel that it was clear yet what God was trying to say.

About two weeks went by and I was sitting in my office, asking the Lord, "okay, what are You trying to say?"

And then it came. I begin to write down my thoughts and it made perfect sense.

"The two bears represent two places in your life, one of contentment (the bear that was eating) and feeding upon the nutrients provided for you (in the Word particularly) and the other place is a place of unpredictability and fear. Embrace that place; kiss the bear. Welcome it for it is a place of faith, and a place of learning. Be like King David who learned how to behave in the cave, who learned how to survive in the desert, to find water, to find food and sustenance, to fight. Kiss the bear."

What a wonderful God to communicate to me that I was about to enter into a time of unpredictability and fear! And, that is exactly what happened. I went through a period of testing and trying at the hands of Christian people (sheep-bite) but through it all, I realized that I was to welcome this time because the Lord was teaching me; the Lord was testing me, and the Lord would sustain me.

I had a fourth dream about a bear some months later. It was a hand-to-paw fight with the creature that was twice my size…but I won. No weapons but my bare hands and I killed the bear. So there was a time to kiss and a time to kill the bear. When it was done, I looked down in my dream and noticed that my legs were all scarred up. I was not in pain, but blood had been spilled, and now I was scarred.

In processing this dream, I realized that I had been wounded in the strength of my legs, the strongest portion of my body. I think the Lord was saying I will have wounds and will bear the marks (no pun intended) of the battle in the strongest part of my ministry at that time. And, that is what took place. But the fact would remain that I won the fight in the strength of the Lord; the bear was defeated and I was to move on.

So, whatever you might be going through, or facing, may seem overwhelming and fearful, but I invite you to *kiss the bear*, to welcome a time like this, because it is in the desert times that God speaks so tenderly to us (Hosea 2:14).

By the way, to cap off this story, God in His humor, planned something just for me to enjoy.

I was in Scotland on a ministry trip some time later when I came across one of those tourist sites that sell various kilts, tartans and swords, plaster your name on key chains, and plaques, showing what the name means and so on. I found the name "Barker" which surprised me somewhat. It was the only one in the entire store, a little cardboard wall hanging that explained the history of the name. I think I actually heard God chuckle when I read that the armorial bearings of the name Barker, was in fact, the head of a bear, well, three of them to be exact, and that reminded me of the three dreams God gave me to warn me of the time to come. I also noted that the head of the bear was decapitated.

I could just imagine God leaning over to Peter and saying, "Watch this Peter; this will be good."

What a setup; just one plaque with Barker on it, in just one store in the middle of the Scottish countryside that I just happen to stop in for a bathroom break and to take a look at souvenirs. Nice touch Lord. You're the best!

Chapter 5
Duh! The Sound of Revelation

...this was not revealed to you by man, but by my Father in heaven.—Matthew 16:17

I'm about to tell you one of the most profound things I have ever heard, or said, and when you hear it, you'll go "Well, duh!"

Are you ready?

You might want to sit down, grab a coffee, breathe a deep breath and really wrap your mind around this. I mean when you hear it and let it sink into your system, you might really launch something new. Your life may never be the same again. This could change the way you do your job, even how you look at life in general. It might even change the way you live, period. Are you ready for it?

I mean if you really get a hold of this, you'll probably never be the same. It's one of those phrases that just sticks to you like peanut butter on bread. I mean...okay, okay, here it is: I mean this was such a revelation to me that I slapped my forehead and said "Well duh!"—okay, okay here it is.

If you always do what you've always done, you'll always get what you've always had.

C'mon, read it again, slowly. Think about it now. Some people go through life and never think to change. One of the definitions of insanity is to continually do the same thing over and over again while expecting a different result. But really, if you always do what you've always done, you'll always get what you've always had.

You might say "Well, duh," and that really is the sound of revelation when it hits your spirit, but if it is so simple, why is it that so many Christians never get out of the flippin' rut they've been in for years? They know the truth of it, yet they still do the same things over and over, and over again. Apparently, a road sign on the Alaskan Highway used to say "be careful how you choose your rut; you'll be in it for the next 200 miles," or something to that effect, and a rut in a Christian life is really a grave with the ends knocked out.

So consider your life. If you don't like what you're getting, try something different. If you don't like your prayer life, try something different, getting up earlier, staying up later, prayer walking, or prayer-journaling, whatever, just do something about it.

If you aren't sensing the Lord's tangible presence in your day to day, get-up-and-go-to-work life, then try something different. If you're a preacher and the well's dry, try something different. It takes risk; it takes faith. We must adjust because if we always do what we've always done, we'll always get what we've always had.

If Abraham didn't risk leaving everything he had ever known to follow after a God he'd just met, history would have been very, very different. But instead against all odds, hope against hope the Bible says, he believed God and it was credited to him righteousness.

What if Zacchaeus had done what he always had instead of climbing up that sycamore tree? What if blind Bartimaeus hadn't risked everything to scream "Jesus, Son of David, have mercy on me!?" What if Gideon decided to stay put and continue grinding wheat in the wine press? What if Jehu decided to ignore Elisha's call, and go on playing cards instead of driving his chariot like a madman and taking out Jezebel? What if Peter hadn't followed the angel out of prison? What if the church hadn't prayed? What if? What if? What if?

What if you don't take the opportunity God is giving you to step out in faith, believe Him and do that thing that He has been talking to you about? If you always do what you've always done, you'll always get what you've always had.

Revelation from God is not complicated.

So often when God speaks to me, He tells me simple truths that when I get them, I think "Well of course...why didn't I see that before?" Then I slap my forehead and say "Duh!"

Revelation is in fact the foundation of how Jesus builds his church. Remember the story in the gospels where Jesus is asking the boys "Guys, who do people say I am?" And, in their brilliance, they responded that some called him a prophet, some Elijah, others Jeremiah. Then he asked them, "Okay, but who do you say I am?"

It was Peter who caught something there, and you can almost see him gasping, pointing at Jesus, and saying "I know, you are the Christ, the Son of the Living God!"

Jesus smiles and winks, and says "Aha! Flesh and blood didn't reveal that to you Peter, but my Father in heaven did. Upon this rock I will build my church and the gates of hell shall not prevail against it!"

Well, of course, a lot of people have mistakenly figured that Peter himself is the rock that Christ was talking about there, because his name means "rock" but I believe the rock Jesus was referring to was the rock of revelatory information, hidden treasures of understanding given by the Father Himself through the Spirit—particularly that knowledge that Jesus is the Son of the Living God!

So how does that work? It's simple. Revelation comes through the Spirit to the spirit. You know that we are triune beings, right? We are created in the image of God, who is Three—Father, Son and Holy Spirit. He designed the Tabernacle for the Israelites to represent that too—outer court, inner court and the holy of holies—three in one. We are also made up of three parts—spirit, soul and body. The soul, which is our mind, our will and emotions, cannot seem to process revelation from the Spirit of God. The soul processes information, processes logic, processes feelings and choices, but the spirit alone—and only one that is quickened by belief in Jesus—is what can really handle revelation from God. Where does God dwell when someone becomes born again? In their spirit. The spirit of a man is where God dwells when you invite Him into your life. As a result, our spirit is always in the presence of the Lord, and it is our spirit that processes His revelation. That's why you can read a Bible passage that you have read for years and then all of a sudden...BAM! The revelation of it hits your spirit, and you never, ever, ever forget it again. That revelation then is worked out through your soul and through your body as you apply it. First there is revelation, and then there's the opportunity to put it into practice.

Take Peter for example who in Acts 10 had a revelatory experience and then the opportunity to put it into practice. He fell into a trance, which by the way, many Christians today would say "Oh that couldn't be God then," and he sees a vision of heaven opened up and something like a large sheet being let down to earth by its four corners. It contained all kinds of four-footed animals and reptiles as well as birds. Then a voice told him "Get up, Peter, kill and eat."

His first response was to the effect of "What? Are you crazy? These are impure, unclean things and I have never eaten anything impure!!"

The voice says—and by the way, the Greek word used for voice here means to disclose, to show, to enlighten or shine—the voice warns Peter not to call anything impure that God has made clean.

This experience happens three times, which makes me relate to Peter as it often takes at least three times before he gets something...three denials, three reinstatements, three visions.

For me it is more like 10 times but we're talking about Peter here. While Peter is still wondering and pondering about this incredible vision of impure vs. pure, the three men that God had already instructed the Gentile Cornelius through an angelic vision to send to Peter (I love it how God works on so many different levels) showed up at his door. He's always doing more behind the scenes than we can see Him doing right in front of our noses.

Peter invites them in, which was already more than a little bit of a no-no in his culture and the next day sets out with them to go to Cornelius' house to share with them the gospel. He must have been thinking all along "This makes no sense whatsoever; I know that I shouldn't be doing this. I can't figure it out. Why would God call something clean when it has already been ruled unclean? But I know that was God…I must be obedient."

So often, we try to figure everything out first before we obey but God usually leads us into the ridiculous, the ludicrous so that we can walk by faith not by sight. We used to sing that old hymn Trust and Obey but lately I've been thinking we might want to change it to Obey and Trust. Obey first; trust the Lord and He'll work everything out.

So Peter had an opportunity to put into practice the word that God was speaking to him. He gave him a revelation that was very new, and now he had to put into practice. Paul says in the letter to the Romans that "Faith comes by hearing, and hearing the word of God." And now after Peter heard the word of God, he needed to walk by faith in it. It was the same in the Old Testament when Joshua was told to march around Jericho, or to have the priests step into the Jordan river—before it would split—or Moses told to stretch out his staff over the Red Sea (I could see him trembling thinking 'this better work!'). Think about Gideon again, David, story after story where people were told something by the Lord, and then they had to act upon it. The scripture says faith comes by hearing, not "having heard." That means it is current; it is now; it is actively hearing the voice of the Lord.

Peter told the gathering at the house that they all know the rules against a Jew associating with a Gentile but then he declares his revelation: "But God has shown me that I should not call any man unclean or impure." If Peter went on what he known from his childhood rather than the current hearing the voice of the Lord, revival never would have happened for the Gentiles.

It wasn't until after Cornelius explains what happened to him, and how God visited him with an angel that Peter exclaimed basically "Now I get it!"

He says "I now realize how true it is that God does not show favoritism but accepts men from every nation who fear him and do what is right."

The rest is remarkable history how the Holy Spirit decides to drop in for a visit there and wreak holy havoc among the believers. He shows up big time and has the Gentiles speaking in tongues and prophesying to the place where there is no point denying what God is doing.

But it was the revelatory work of the Holy Spirit that softened Peter's heart, allowing himself to even walk with a Gentile, and then later to step foot into one's home and share the good news of the Lord Jesus Christ. Peter put feet to his faith.

God is very, very sneaky. I respectfully call Him Jehovah Sneaky these days. Perhaps there is a clue that God had something up His sleeve when you consider that Peter was staying at a tanner's house. Hmmm, that was a cultural no-no as well! Seems God was already softening up his heart for a mighty move. And, you know what, God really does like to speak with us and teach us how to walk in faith. He has given us the Holy Spirit to guide and lead us into all truth. He is so good to us! He will take us into tough situations so that we can adjust in faith. He so likes it when we act in faith. I heard someone say recently that God allows things to happen TO us so that things can happen IN us, so that things can happen THROUGH us.

But while He has been sneaky with me, more often He has just had to talk straight to me and that is like being hit in the side of the head with my own thick, leather-bound Bible. Once I was going through a season of yuck, which I think is a Greek word meaning crap and I wasn't seeing clearly; I was frustrated; I was angry, and tired; I was distracted and drained.

Then God in His graciousness spoke a revelatory word directly to my spirit. I actually knew the information before in my soul but it wasn't going deep into my core.

He said, ***"Rick, Satan hates you. He hates you and he hates everything you're doing in the kingdom. He hates you with a deep hatred and he wants to take you out."***

Wow! Simple enough alright, but this came at a time when I was wondering why I was going through what I was going through. I had forgotten that I am in a war. I was focused on the wrong things, at the wrong times, and when the realization came that this in fact is a war, I took the revelation and did something about it. I rallied the troops together; I called for prayer and great breakthrough came. Again, it was the revelatory word of God spoken, and then an opportunity to put feet to it, to do something about it, to obey.

So, if you always do what you've always done, you'll always get what you've always had. If Peter had dismissed the revelation and had always done what he always had, breakthrough would not have come to the Gentile church. In fact, most of us would not be in the kingdom today.

If you're tired of what you're getting, get something new by trying something different. Step out. Step out in faith. God likes that and He will meet you in that very moment.

Chapter 6
Ready or Not Here I Come…

All the ways of the Lord are loving and faithful for those who keep the demands of His covenant. —Psalm 25:10

I had my sermon all prepared.

I mean I hadn't preached in about four weeks and had been really working on this one. It was called "Ready or not, here I come." I even had it printed in the bulletin. I'm not usually a three-point sermonator but it even had three points to ponder about how God surprises us sometimes. First point was about the return of Christ. When is He coming back? Your response should be "soon!" Right. So, I was going to talk about the return of Christ in the first point, Matthew 24, and 25 about the way the world is shaping up but we're not to be frightened. There is a date set; there will be a marriage supper of the Lamb; there will be a wedding. It will happen. God will do as His word declares. God has it all under control. So ready or not, here I come—that was point number one.

Point number two was how He is about to come to the corporate church, based on the letters to the seven churches in Revelation and how in almost all of them He says "I will come to you." But He is talking about a coming that is one of judgment and it is a bit scary because He says He will come and remove our lamp-stand unless we start dealing with some things in our lives, such as the idolatry which He referred to when He spoke about the Nicolaitans. I was going to get my wife, Marci, to share about some thoughts she had on crafted images that people struggle with in their lives that are ungodly, and how God was saying "Ready or not, here I come" in regards to idolatry. She has amazing revelation from the Lord on some of these things and I love to hear her speak.

Point three was going to be about our personal lives, and how God does a sneak attack and comes to us and surprises us when we least expect Him. Even in the return of the Lord, He says at a time when you don't expect Him, He'll come. I considered the guys on the road to Emmaus and how Jesus walked with them when they weren't expecting Him to, and how they didn't even recognize Him until He disappeared. Suuurprise!

So I had all this prepared, and then He came, and did that very thing! He surprised me with His presence on the Friday before the sermon, and I began to get this phrase that pounded my spirit over and over again, and the more I thought about it, the more revelatory it became to me and it built my faith. It's about God not being taken by surprise by anything or anyone but that indeed He has the whole world in His hands. So I chucked out the three-point sermon and delivered this word: **The story's not over until it's over, until God says it's over, and God will have the last laugh.**

I just think of the dozens of stories in the scriptures where God seems to enjoy having the last laugh on his enemies. From the first pages of Genesis right through to Revelation, in nearly every chapter, the truth of the statement "It's not over till God says so" comes through. No matter what you go through, no matter what can be thrown at you, the story is not over till it's over, until God says it's over, and you know what, He will have the last laugh.

He is so confident in His ability. Our circumstances seem so big, so impossible but they are trivial for the Lord.

When they were teenagers, I took my kids, Dustin and Denai to a small community just outside of Calgary Alberta on a ministry trip. We did some practical things like digging an irrigation ditch, some ministry stuff on the streets and we helped with a church plant outreach effort.

During one of the days, my 14-year daughter noticed in a shop window a pair of running shoes that were so 'in' that she just had to have them. She begged me with puppy dog eyes and that little pout face, saying "Puhllleeeeeaassee, Dad?"

Well being the good dad that I want to be, I really wanted to get them for her, and being the smart husband I long to be, I immediately telephoned home to ask my wife about it. She said "Go for it."

So together Denai and I went to the store, her almost giddy, but that would be uncool so she was just really happy. We got there, and to her utter devastation, the shoes were too small, and they were the only pair the store had.

I remembered the silence as we walked back to the car. She was so bummed out and had that look on her face that seemed to say "Nothing ever works out for me."

I figured that we'll probably stop at another store somewhere and they'll likely have them, so I smiled and said to Denai, "Hey, the story's not over." We prayed about it and left it at that.

Well, we didn't find any in Alberta or B.C. and so we came home when we did, empty-handed.

At home, the phone rang for Denai. It was one of our youth interns who called to say that she had some brand new shoes for her to try because they were too small for her. You guessed it…same shoes.

Now as that good father, I thought "teachable moment" and I said to my daughter "Don't ever think the story is over until it is over."

Think of Jericho tightly shut up, the citizens of Jericho laughing outrageously at the Israelites from the top of the massive walled city. The Israelites quietly marched around the city, looking like complete idiots, until they shouted at the right time and as a result the walls came crashing down. God had the last laugh on that occasion.

Ask Job. I mean he must have thought it was over when he lost everything and then started breaking out in boils. Was the story over? Nope. The story wasn't over because God was still on the job (no pun intended) and He turned all the cursing into an abundant blessing and He gave him double portion of all that he had.

Think of ol' Gideon there counting his numbers thinking he might have a chance even though the odds were four to one. Then God tells him to pare down the army until the odds are now 400 to one. Then God gave the instructions to take a pitcher, a torch and a trumpet and wait for the right time to obey the command to break the pitcher, shout a shout and wave the flame. Who had the last laugh? God did once again, as fear struck the enemy's camp and a great victory was won for the Lord.

Think about David facing Goliath, the huge Philistine warrior who laughed when he saw the ruddy teenager come out to fight him with a sling.

Think of Moses, a stutterer, being told to go and deliver the people of Israel from the mightiest man on the planet..."And oh, Moses, just a minute...here's a stick."

Think of Lazarus quite dead in the tomb. I mean, it looked pretty over! But the story wasn't over, nope, not until God said it was over and He would have the last laugh.

Just ask Peter. He must have thought the story was over. I mean he denied Christ three times, denied even knowing the man! He cursed. Was the story over? No! Jesus came and reinstated him three times.

Ask Paul. He was stoned, beaten up, in jail, left for dead, shipwrecked. Was the story over? Not until God said so.

Ask Jonah in the belly of a whale. Was the story over?

Think of the widow's oil that flowed until there was no more emptiness to be filled; think of Samson wiping out more enemies in his death than he did in his life, think of the jealous peers of Daniel who snickered when the king had to throw Daniel into the lions den, only to end up there themselves when God saved Daniel from the pride's late-night snack.

Look at David, anointed king over all Israel. What happened right after that? He was living in the caves for many years! He must have thought, "Well, that word was really off!" He must have thought the story was pretty much over, but it wasn't because God had a plan and He was working His plan. He laughs at our plans, but He is working His plan.

Go back to the beginning when Adam and Eve fell in the garden, and sinned. They must have thought the story was over. But God gave them a promise that her seed would crush the enemy serpent. So there was hope. But think of what it must have been like to be escorted out of the garden.

They had a promise from God and as someone once said "If you have the promise of God, you have the reality."

So here Eve gets pregnant and bears Cain. At the beginning they must have believed he was that seed, the promised one of God who would crush the serpent's head. He was just a baby, but why wouldn't they think he was the one. Then he got a little older, and they began to wonder. He has some character deficits, a little arrogant, a little rude at times and talk about selfish!

Cain. His name even means "man" and I think he represents the ways of man, trying to work our way into salvation, please Him by our own works. Then Abel came along. Now, hey, Abel was tender in his heart; he loved God, maybe he was the promise! And, then Cain murders Abel! Think of how Eve must have felt. Downtrodden, in despair, she wondered if the story was over. But no, the story wasn't over because God gave them Seth.

Cain represents man, Abel represents the death of Christ and as I thought about it, I realized the Seth represents the resurrection! New beginnings and a new season came about for Adam and Eve. In fact, when you look at the genealogies, Cain fades out, Abel didn't have a chance to have genealogy but it is Seth in Luke 2 who is recorded in the history of Jesus—Seth, the son of Adam! He was the one to carry that promise for Eve and for Adam. The story wasn't over, even when there was death, pain and trouble, He brings a Seth into our lives, a new beginning, a new time.

I think of Abraham as good as dead when He was given the promise of Isaac. I mean, he looked at Sarah his wife, thinking "How can this ever happen? We are old and gravity is taking over. Look at us!" Then Sarah gets the idea of giving Hagar to Abraham (man's ways) but God had a plan and He worked His plan and Sarah got pregnant with Isaac and God had the last laugh. Isaac's name even means laughter. But if you read further in Genesis in chapter 25 after Sarah died, you can marvel with me. We just understood that Abraham was basically dead in his body and couldn't produce any children but God intervened and Isaac was born. But now after Sarah died, we read in Genesis 25 that old Abraham took another wife whose name was Keturah who gave him another six children! Yup, six! Hey, the story's not over till it's over and when God wants to have the last laugh, look out! Six more kids! Way to go, God!

He is so faithful. He is so generous. He has us in His hands. Do not worry. Come to Him and allow Him to draw near to you. Let faith rise in you because God is right there in the midst of your storm, in the midst of your trial.

Early in our marriage, I was jobless and a government error (they did admit it) had caused my unemployment insurance cards to be filed out of order and so the money was not coming in. My son was just a toddler and we needed food, and I was angry.

I would walk to the post office, stick the key into our box, turn it in great hope, only to see an empty compartment staring back at me. I would then slam the door shut in frustration because nothing was there. I would have to think of something to say to my poor wife who was at home anticipating some kind of breakthrough in our financial situation. By the way, there is very little satisfaction in slamming a post office box door—it hardly even makes a noise!

The stress that this whole thing brought was huge. I remember walking through the door and seeing my wife sitting on the floor with our son, looking up at me with hopeful eyes. I shook my head no.

At this point in our life, we were on the edge of serving God. We had made a commitment but we did not get to church often because I had no vehicle; I didn't like hitching rides with others; I was unemployed. I hated my life.

I grabbed the Bible off the table and these words came out of my mouth: "Do we chuck this thing?"

I actually did; I threw it onto the floor. But even as I chucked it, I realized it was our only hope that somehow, some way God would come through. Right in that moment, Marci and I got down on our knees beside our bed, and I remember praying through tears "God, this is probably the place you wanted us all along…"

The next day I went to the post office box abounding with faith. I was so pumped. I knew today was the day of my provision! I turned the key in the box, opened the door and there it was…absolutely nothing!

I almost died right there on the spot. I was so confused! I slowly closed the door and walked away toward home. On the way home, God gave me a revelatory word, actually two words. He usually speaks that way to me, one and two words at a time. I'm thick.

He spoke into my spirit *"Remember Gideon."*

That was all. It came strongly in the depths of my spirit, though.

So I started to remember Gideon. God pared his army down so that only God could get the glory for a victorious battle against a huge army. The odds were stacked against Gideon but God came through.

Perhaps God was bringing me to this place where only He would get the glory for providing for me, not the government, not social services (they had already refused me as well due to the fact I was already supposed to be on unemployment insurance) not my own ability, but God. So I went home with that word and hoped that maybe it would help even Marci to have some hope.

Do you know that in less than two hours I was standing dumbfounded in my living room with more money in my hand than I would have had, even if my check would have arrived? I didn't even leave the house! Several of God's people had come by, knocked at the door and said "God told me to give you this" and handed me $94, another one $46 and so on. I couldn't believe it.

This was nothing to God. But He graciously used it to teach me a mighty lesson. Our God is able to make all grace abound to you so that in all things, at all times, having all that you need, you will abound to every good work. (2 Corinthians 9:8)

He's so majestic, so brilliant. He can change a nation in a day. He can change your situations, and my situations in a moment. Nothing is too difficult for Him. Only believe.

Think of it. Think of the greatest laugh God ever had, when His enemy, Satan, thought he finally had gotten rid of the Son of God by having Him crucified on the cross and stuck in a hole in the ground. Satan thought then, "HA! The story's over buddy! You lose!"

Whoops! Suuuurprise! The stone was rolled away and Jesus came striding out in tumultuous victory! What an awesome God!

Yes, it looked over, but it is never over, my friends, until God says it's over, and He will have the last laugh!

And just a thought...even when we die as Christians, the story is not over; the adventure is just beginning. For the Christian, the story is never over.

Chapter 7
Living Life from the Inside Out

For those who are led by the Spirit of God are the sons of God.
— Romans 8:14

There are four kinds of people in the world today.

Those who make things happen.

Those who watch things happen.

Those who wonder what just happened.

And the fourth kinds of people are those who watch God make things happen and stand back in awe and wonder.

I want to be in the fourth category, just watching what God is doing, joining Him in that work and seeing His wonders.

When you see a sign in a restaurant window that says Under New Management, what kind of things does that bring up in your mind? Better food, better service? Renovations? You bet. I think every Christian should be given a sign like that when they become born again. Here's your sign...Under New Management.

God's in the house and He's renovating. God is busy changing things and in fact, the old nature, the old sinful man has lost his job and there is a new manager!

What happens when you ask Jesus to come and live in your heart? We know a tiny little man does not come in and set up shop; He doesn't come in a physical way. You might recall the illustrations used a great deal in the 80s of the little chair in your heart, signifying the throne of your life, and Jesus sitting on it. Sometimes we push Him off the throne and the big "I" is sitting on it. That's a helpful illustration. But what really takes place in our being when we say "yes" to the Lordship of Christ in our life?

Before conversion, we are going through life bound to this earth, dead to God in our spirit, miserable in our emptiness, void of God, generally unhappy campers. Something is missing in our life. God has created you with a God-shaped vacuum that is inside you—it really is a mystery—inside you that can only be filled by God, a place where God alone can dwell.

After conversion, it's different. Something's changed. There's a spring in your step; your spirit comes alive; you're no longer bound to this earth, there's a Bible in your hand, a joy in your heart, and a sparkle in your eye.

How did it happen? The scripture gives insight in I Thessalonians 5:23 about who we are as human beings created in the image of God. We are a tripartite person. We have three parts, a spirit, soul and body. Everybody does. We are created as spiritual beings first and we have a soul and a body. Each of the three is also made up of three parts—as the psalmist said we are "fearfully and wonderfully made."

The Spirit consists of Communion, Conscience and Wisdom; the Soul is made up of Mind, Will and Emotions, and the Body, of course, is made up of Blood, Bone and Flesh.

Jesus comes and dwells in us. Where? He doesn't dwell in our body, or our soul. He is spirit John 4:24 says and He dwells in our spirit. It is our spirit that is eternal. We are a step above the animal world; that is why we don't see animals coming into church to find out more about Jesus. When we tell our dogs to heel, they don't stand up with their front paw out praying for someone to be touched. They don't have a spirit. We have a spirit; we are different.

Our body—well that's obvious. There's a physical part to us that gives us our world awareness, our five senses, our seeing, our hearing, our smell, our touch, our taste. We are in a physical "tent" as the apostle Paul calls it, but it is not "us". If my arms are chopped off, I'm still me. I'm still who I am because the essence of who I am is inside.

Part of that is our soul—mind, will and emotions—which is our self awareness. It is about what we feel, what we think, our choices, or will. We are a feeling, decision-making, thinking being.

Then there's our spirit, which the Bible also calls the secret place, our innermost being where we get God-awareness, and revelation. What takes place in our spirit, affects our mind, will and emotions, and our body.

We are created in the image of God, one whole being but like Him, we are three in one—body, soul, and spirit. And we are constantly changing both inside and out, from glory to glory, from faith to faith, and from victory to victory.

On the outside, the body changes and it might be more noticeable. We stand on the scale and suck in our gut. Our spouse says "That won't help" and we respond "Oh yes it will — now I can see the numbers on the scale…so there."

The spirit is where God dwells. It's eternal. Before asking Christ into our life, before He comes and quickens our spirit, we are spiritually dead, and barren of that eternal life. Our spirit though is not inactive before conversion. In fact, people are very active spiritually, but they are not made alive until the Spirit of God touches them and brings them to real life. Remember that movie when the little boy says "I see dead people"…well we all see dead people every day because their spirit is yet to have come alive in Jesus Christ. They walk around in suits and ties, and work in buildings and live in homes, but spiritually, they are dead until Christ makes them alive through faith in Him.

And, when He does quicken our spirit and make us alive, He comes and dwells in our spirit. Living life from the inside out is learning to live life by the Spirit of God, learning to keep stride with the Spirit in the midst of battle, learning to step back into the place of the Spirit where you can see things from God's perspective.

Jesus said that which is born of flesh is flesh and that which is born of spirit is spirit.

That is what happens every Sunday morning in churches all over the world. You basically pull your soul and body into alignment with your spirit. That is why people respond by saying "Wow, it felt so good to be in His presence."

Well, we are always in His presence right? Where does He dwell? In your spirit. When we come into His presence, we are actually stepping into that place of the spirit. We bring our mind, our will and our emotions into alignment with the Spirit of God. Our spirit is always in the presence of God for that is where He dwells. As a Christian, your spirit has no other focus than abiding in the presence of God; the presence of the Lord is there and we must learn to step into it.

It's easier to do this at church with a bunch of believers, but we need to do this every day, whether we are in a secular vocation working among pre-Christians, at a ministry-type job, or just in our car, at our house, at school—wherever!

As a journalist I use to head to work in the morning thanking God for my job and asking Him to use me as much as possible during the day. I recall time after time of doing interviews when all of a sudden, the person I was interviewing would say something that would trigger my spirit and I would know that something was happening in the kingdom realm. I would put my pen and paper down and put my pad to the side and just talk to them. Many times there were open doors for sharing my faith and opportunities to pray with people, even Members of Parliament who found themselves unloading their stuff on me, despite the fact that I was a journalist! As I listened, the people would pour out his or her life and we would end up praying together. God granted great favor with government officials, police, municipal authorities, and school officials. Why? Because the Lord was present and where He is, is holy.

I would pray for favor and inspiration in writing stories. I would pray "God I know that You have inspired writers before (Duh! The Bible) so would you inspire me as I write?" And He would because I stepped into that place of the spirit before writing. Do you think God is a good writer? Could He come up with a good lead to a story?

It became easy because I allowed Him to be in my every day life. It has happened in stores, in coffee shops, on street corners, picking up hitch-hikers. I mean you probably relate to that feeling of being in a grocery store in the produce department when all of a sudden, a lady begins to share with you her story and you find yourself ministering to her and thinking "Gee, all I wanted was some bananas." But He gave you some fruit of a different kind.

And that is living life from the inside out.

In the Old Testament the Holy Spirit was poured out upon individuals for particular times on particular people for a specific task but in New Testament times He is being poured out on all flesh! And He is in you, so release Him out!

We often pray "Pour out Your spirit" and I understand the heart in that but He has been poured out. I think we need to let Him out of us because He dwells in us now and Jesus said "Out of your innermost being will flow rivers of living water" referring to the Holy Spirit. He is crying out "LET ME OUT!"

It's not so much a coming down but a coming out of. I heard one speaker say that to be thirsty for God sounds spiritual but it is really quite silly because Jesus said "If you come to me, you'll never thirst again."

All you have to do is learn how to get a drink, and it is from within, for Jesus dwells within by His Spirit. Go draw deeply from the well of salvation within you.

So how do we do that?

It begins in worship, in praise, in abiding in thanksgiving. We can do that wherever we are, on our way to work or school or wherever. We need to keep an attitude of gratitude, an attitude of worship wherever we are.

Think of Paul and Silas in the jail at midnight, chained up, rats running around, all damp and dark, cold and clammy. And Paul leans over to his buddy, who is barely awake and says "Hey, you wanna sing?"

"Okay...uh, what do you want to sing?"

"I don't know, how about *This is the Day*?"

They begin to praise and as they praise, BOOM! The earthquake happens and the church in Phillipi was born.

What if they hadn't? What if they just whined and complained about their trial like most people do?

In the midst of a trial, God is at work. He is continually trying to teach you about Himself.

What you need from Him, He wants to teach you about.

He uses trials to break things in us, particularly the tendency to live our lives soulishly with our mind, our will and emotions.

We're really bad about this in the western world. It is all rationalistic thinking and yet God says "Don't lean unto your own understanding but trust in the Lord with all your heart and He will direct your paths."

That's so hard. We're always leaning unto our own understanding. That's what gets us into trouble. God says "Step back into the place of the spirit, our secret place; step back into Me and I will direct you. Get things from My perspective."

Now, your soul is not your enemy. Your soul even desires to serve God but so often when it does, it becomes legalistically doing stuff to work your way into a better relationship with God. It's religious gobbley-gook at its worst. It's works, works, works, doing, doing, doing, instead of simply being. And, as a result, you get worn out just trying to juggle everything in your life through your mind, will and emotions. It goes back to the Garden and going to the wrong tree, the tree of knowledge of good and evil rather than the Tree of Life.

Living life from the inside out is from the Spirit. There is rest there, and peace there; there is joy there. There is balance when you have your soul living under the direction of your spirit, where God Himself calls the shots.

Your soul will rule your life to ruin if you let it. That's why people go up and down like a yo-yo.

"I'm feeling depressed, so I'm depressed."

"I don't feel like worshiping so I won't. I don't want to be a hypocrite."

Since when did feelings have the throne? That's why David said "Bless the Lord O my soul!" He was bringing his soul into alignment and making it obedient.

He took charge and said to his body "Lift your hands and worship."

Your soul processes logic but God always asks us to do things that are illogical! Think of the scriptural stories, which we have already talked about—Gideon and his great victory with a picture and a flame, Joshua at Jericho, David and Goliath. Your soul doesn't process the illogical well; we argue, and we try to figure out and lean on our own understanding.

But God wants you to lean on Him and His ways, His perspective, His walk of faith.

Your spirit processes revelation when God speaks. It drops into your spirit and goes deep inside beyond the rational even.

Your spirit uses your soul and body for processing things but I think most Christians live in the soulish realm most of the time. Even many of our songs are soulish—which in and of itself is not bad, but it cannot define us.

When you worship, you become God-conscious. You come into His rest, His fullness is there. Peace comes, and you can do that—step into the place of the Spirit—any where, any time, any place.

The fact is, you do need to position yourself in order to receive revelation from God. Expect God to speak. Ask Him to speak. Position yourself to receive from Him through your worship, adoration and praise of God.

I'll give you an example of God speaking in a way that seem impossible but what I am about to say next may seem strange to you because it was to me. I was on a prayer walk in a small community outside of Glasgow, Scotland on a beautiful night and the Lord revealed some things to me in a manner that "totally weirded me out" if you know what I mean. In fact, I quenched it and shut it down and it wasn't until I came back to Canada and thought about it some more that I realized what was happening.

During this walk, I was passing by small homes on a road to my destination, a high place overlooking the village. As I went by the homes, I was praying for the people that lived there. I didn't know them; I knew nothing of them. I was just praying for blessing. Then I felt the strong presence of the Lord and heard His voice saying "Do you want to know how to pray for these people?"

"Sure Lord," I responded but wasn't really thinking too much about it.

As I walked and prayed I began to notice things flooding my mind, words such as "This family is a Christian family; they actually love Me very much but they are in a church that is struggling..."

Up the road, more words, "This man is abusive to his kids..."

As I listened I was praying for each home but then it began to get to me and I thought "Wait a minute; I can't know these things. What am I doing? This is too weird!"

Unfortunately, as I look back now, I realize that I started praying about other things and actually quenched His spirit. But what was happening was that I was stepping into God's perspective of things; He was funneling things to me to help me pray more effectively. Perhaps it would have increased even, to the place of going up to a door, knocking on it and asking to be of assistance in prayer. Who knows? I don't...because I had shut it down. And, I have since repented of that.

Paul said "It is not me who lives, but Christ in me!" There are exciting things that can take place when we let Him out. Just release Him to be Himself in you. It is not that Christ is in us so we can copy Him, or Christ in us to help us, but in fact it is Christ in us, instead of us! It is the great exchange! He lives through us by faith. Wow!

Christ is living in me, through me! It is an amazing mystery, but what a joyful experience!

Watchman Nee said "Say to God, I can't do this, but Your life in me can and will. The law of Christ in you will always work, always; we need to rest in it. When we realize that Christ Himself is our life and we don't need willpower, we look to Him who is in us. The victory is His, and so therefore ours. Christ Himself is our life, empowering and dwelling in us."

Living life from the inside out is not living a life that is impossible, or forcing ourselves to be holy. When you're speaking to someone, ask Jesus what He would say if He was standing there, because He is!

Everything that is demanded of you as a Christian is possible because Christ is in you. We don't need to be a superstar, we just need to be available. We don't have to be experienced before stepping out in faith believing God wants to use us. Jesus first sent out the disciples two by two when they had very little training.

I remember the story of Helen, a little old lady from Seattle who wanted to share her faith with young people so she would walk down to the University of Seattle and speak to the students there as they came and went. She had seven purses stolen during that time, so she's thinking about this. She was 74 years old at the time but she got the idea that this could be a ministry for her. She now lets people steal her purse. She gets all kinds of purses. She goes down with one thing in her purse, a little New Testament and a note that says "I'm very sorry that you must be so troubled that you need to steal my purse but God loves you and so do I so if you need help, you can call me at this number." And she put her phone number on it.

She was 74 years old, but she saw an opportunity and she took it.

Be available. Step out.

Our soul says "Well when I have more money, or more time then I'll step out."

Our spirit says "Whatever Father, here I am, send me."

We need to step back, live life from the inside out and see the wonders of God.

Sometimes people have trouble with the thought of God speaking to us apart from His written word but let me say that while He does indeed speak, He will never, ever go against His written word. He speaks in many ways so we need to unstop that well inside us, the well that contains His life-giving Spirit.

We do that through repentance. If there's a log of bitterness inside your well, take it out and unstop the well of life. If there's sin inside, deal with it; take it out and get rid of it and let the water flow.

Live life from the inside out. Step back into that secret place of the spirit, see things from God's perspective; join Him in His work and you'll have that sparkle in your eye, that spring in your step and people will ask you for the good news.

Chapter 8
S'cuse Me but I'm Drowning Here

Let us go over to the other side... —Mark 4:35

Did you ever notice that God always brings us into impossible situations?

I mean 'always' is a brittle word, a strong word, but I think it fits. I did extensive study on the word always, and yup, it means always. He always leads us into places of whacked out impossibilities and stacked-up odds against us. He is amazing. He is faithful. But He will ALWAYS bring you into impossible situations. Why? Because He wants you to learn to trust Him and Him alone to be all you ever need.

Think of Moses having been a shepherd for 40 years in the middle of nowhere, having God speak to him and say "Go deliver my people." Impossible against mighty pharaoh! But not for ALMIGHTY God! It seemed that Moses spent the first 40 years of his life thinking he was *the man,* and that he could even accomplish great things for God his way—like killing the Egyptian. But then he spent the next 40 years learning that he really was nothing. Then God used the last 40 years of his life to show how He can use a nothing and make something totally spectacular happen. God loves humility.

Think of Shadrach, Meshach and Abednego. Talk about an

impossible situation! I mean they were actually in the fire! But once again, God comes through.

Think of David running out against a guy nine feet tall who was wearing a headdress that made him appear another three or four feet taller—and he was threatening the youngster, telling him he's going to be fed to the birds!

Think of Paul and over 200 guys ship-wrecked, some who didn't even know how to swim. All of them are saved from drowning because they heed the word of God in the middle of an impossible situation.

Think of the disciples in the boat screaming "Lord do you even care if we drown?!!"

So often, He is the 11th hour, 59th minute God. He waits till the last possible moment to rescue us.

But even if He doesn't rescue us, we will serve Him. That's what the three Hebrew teens said before being thrown in the fire. "Even if our God does not save us, we will worship only Him."

The youth at our church used to say "If they beat us up, God will heal us. If they kill us, we'll be with God, so get pumped up!"

There is so much in that story in Mark 4 about Jesus in a boat asleep in the stern in the middle of the storm.

You see He had said to the disciples "Let's go over to the other side." I'm not even sure He knew there was going to be a storm but He only did what the Father told Him, so when the Father says "Let's go over to the other side" they are going over to the other side, storm or no storm. That's why He could sleep.

First of all, I would say that Jesus is always saying to us "Let's go over." It might be to the other side, or here or there, but He is always on the move in our life. And He's not going 'under,' He's going over! He leads us from a place of victory not defeat. There is always movement and mobility, motion and flexibility. He is continually shaping us into the word that He spoke over us—oh my goodness, there's another chapter! He speaks words over us prophetically, words of destiny and anointing, which totally launches things in us—and then He shapes us into the very word He spoke over us. And, that my friends, is going over to the other side. We learn things in the going over. We grow. We gain faith.

The scripture says that "Leaving the crowd behind, they took Him along, just as He was, in the boat" (verse36).

Right off the bat we see that in following Jesus there is a leaving behind that takes place. You must leave the crowd behind when you follow Him. Did you ever notice that the closer Jesus got to the day of crucifixion, the more He seemed to make it harder for people to follow? He increasingly said things that would cause offense and questioning, such as "He who does not hate his father and mother is not worthy to be called my disciples," and "You have to count the cost in following me," "Eat my flesh, drink my blood," "Deny yourself, take up your cross daily," and much, much more. It is not an easy thing to follow Christ; it goes against the grain of society, against the natural—because it is supernatural even to follow Him. There is a real leaving that takes place.

The Bible says that in marriage there is a leaving, a cleaving and a weaving that occurs. "For this reason a man shall leave his father and mother, cleave unto his own wife, and the two shall become one flesh" (Genesis 2:24). It is unhealthy for a married couple to not leave a father and mother, continually clinging on to the old way of life. In our relationship with Christ, there is also a leaving that takes place, a cleaving unto Him, and in fact, it is His desire is that we become one with Him.

Secondly the story says that they took Him along just as He was. I never noticed the phrase 'just as he was' until recently. What does that mean? So often, I think we have a distorted picture of Jesus. For some He is the meek, mild weakling Jesus that is depicted in some artists' renditions as effeminate. For some He is seen more like the distant president or director of the universe. They'd recognize Him maybe if they saw Him, but there's no relationship. For others He is the Lion, the angry Jesus who flips tables and makes a whip to confront sinners.

But those disciples took Jesus just as He was. We have to take Him into our boat, just as He is. He is both the Lion and the Lamb. He is gentle, but He is also the consuming fire, both meek and mighty, innocent, jealous and kind, righteous and lowly, humble and with blazing eyes of fire. We must take Him as He is, not our distorted Jesus, or the one who doesn't confront, or on the other hand, the one who does not love. He is the expression of the Father, all of Him. Are you ready for that?

So back to the boat...You know there were at least four trained fishermen in that boat that day, and all of them are terrified, fighting for their lives because the waves were buffeting the boat with a fury. You almost have to wonder if this storm was produced supernaturally by the enemy to destroy them. Finally one of them gets enough courage to wake him up, probably Peter, and asks him if He cares if they drown. I don't think that was a quiet polite Canadian question. I think it was bang-the-fist-on-the-dashboard kind of burst-out-loud rant like HELLO! DON'T YOU CARE IF WE DROWN?!!!!

Ever been there? Ever feel like you're about to lose it? Ever lose it? Ever cry out "Jesus! Don't you even care? Do you see me down here? Do you hear me?"

And then in His time, He answers you in some way that you didn't expect and you sheepishly [good word] say "Oops, sorry Lord."

Those disciples were fully enrolled in the real Jesus School, and at this point were actually failing, which gives all of us hope, eh.

When Jesus stood up, wiped His eyes and commanded the winds and the waves to "BE STILL!" a lesson was about to be given. Yep, here it comes. They looked around them. Right in front of their eyes, the waves rock their way to the flatness of glass; the winds simply cease and the squall is totally gone. As they were sitting there wiping the water from their faces, I can hear them saying "Oh.my...God!"

And, I can see Jesus smiling and turning to them saying, "Exactly!"

He then asks them two questions, two deep penetrating questions, which is very common for Him. He asks "Why were you so afraid?"

"What?! S'cuse me, but we were drowning right here in the boat!"

Another may have cried out "C'mon Jesus, we were going to die! I can still taste the water in my mouth; we're drenched here! Look, there's a fish in my pocket!"

But the key word in that question is the smallest one of the bunch—the word 'so'. Why were you *so* afraid? Fear is not always a bad thing. Fear is like the indicator light on your dashboard saying "Hello up there, time to do something!" But the Lord always says "Do not fear." In the original Hebrew language, it would have read do not DO fear.

Fear comes, and fear causes a reaction. Our reaction in the boat in the middle of a storm, should be to rise up in the face of fear, full of faith in the One who saves. Most of the time though, if you're like me, the first reaction is a far cry from the calm, confident, peaceful response. It is more like the disciples' wail of "Don't you care?!"

The second question He asks is "Where is your faith?" It's like Jesus was saying "Don't you get it? Don't you know who I am? I only do what the Father says, and upon His word I move. I am with you. I said we were going to the other side so we're going to the other side. Trust me. Faith guys, it's all about faith. Without it, you can't even please the Father."

The fact of the matter is that right in the middle of our raging storm, when everything else is screaming out in opposition, He simply wants us to get it. Get it? Trust Him! He is with you in your boat!

So the sea has calmed down. Life is good. Immediately they come to the other side. Must have been a Holy Ghost outboard motor or the angels stepped in and whisked them to the other side. Wow. Imagine now the guys laughing and elbowing one another.

"I wasn't afraid; you were afraid!"

"Shuddup! I was totally fine. It was James and John who were doin' all the yellin'." Ah, boys will be boys eh.

Laughter and joyful jostling. The boat eases into the beach with that familiar crunching wood-on-sand sound and the laughter is suddenly drowned out with another new sound.

A man, a stark naked man, comes running out of the bushes onto the beach, screaming at the top of his lungs, arms flailing. Did I mention he's naked. He's totally demonized. "Aaaaahhhhhhhhhrrrg!! What are you doing here?! What do you want with me, Jesus, Son of the Most High God swear to God you won't torture me!" He's screeching at the top of his voice.

I can hear the disciples' thoughts, can't you?

"Right. Okay, I think I'll just stay in my comfortable little boat thanks. That's alright. I'll just sit here."

Can you see the ways of God? Can you see that one victorious moment, one lesson from Jesus, often leads us right into the sheer impossibility of the next one? That's how we grow; that's how we increase in our faith, one step at a time, daily into new things. From glory to glory He is changing us. That's an awful wonderful thought if you get my drift, a scary, exciting time.

Jesus totally sets the man free. Here he is hanging out at the tombs, chained and bound, out of his mind and Jesus sets him free. It's kind of a picture of the church sometimes isn't it? Hanging around death and dead things, dead religion, dead tradition, bound and chained to man's ways, not free at all, not even in our right minds so to speak. Then Jesus comes and sets us free. The next scene shows the man, sitting with Jesus, in his right mind, new set of clothes and totally free. He ends up going home and spreading the good news, which is also what the church is supposed to do. Another impossible situation taken care of by the precious and magnificent Son of God.

I heard someone say once that the miracle wasn't so much in the calming of the storm as it was in the calming of the man.

At any moment Jesus can calm the storm around you, silence it with just a word, but more importantly, He wants to calm the storm within you, help you learn how to trust in Him right in the midst of the impossibilities surrounding your life.

If you look through the driving rain, if you strain to see through the winds, wiping the rain and water from your eyes, you'll see Him. Yup, there He is. He is striding across the deck of your ship so to speak; He's walking right toward you, and He has a smile on His face. It's joyful and all-confident. He has something tucked under His arm that you can't make out yet. As He gets closer, He laughs as the boat rocks His step a little. He's not worried. Nothing takes Him by surprise. He's your hero. He's your champion and He's coming right to you! As He reaches you, He deftly swings out what is under His arm. It's a blanket, a picnic blanket! He throws it out in front of you and quickly you remember "He sets a table before me in the presence of my enemies" (Psalm 23:5) and you realize everything is going to be okay.

I'm reminded of one of the most memorable moments in recent Olympic history. It took place in 1992, at the summer Olympic Games in Barcelona, Spain. A British runner named Derek Redman had been through 22 surgeries after an injury he suffered while getting ready for the 400 meter race in the 1988 Olympics in Seoul. Yet there he was competing. People were amazed that he was running again, let alone being in the Olympics representing his country. The gun goes. The runners bolted. He was in the middle of the pack of some of the fastest runners in the world when, about halfway around the track, he pulled his hamstring and wiped out.

Of course, everyone thought he was done; the broadcasters started yelling, "Derek Redman is out of the race! Derek Redman is out of the race!" The cameraman stayed with the rest of the runners as they finished the race, but then raced back to Derek Redman who was still down on the track, trying to pull himself back up. He was determined to finish the race!

It seemed that the crowd forgot about the winner and turned to watch this great athlete slowly stand up and hobble around the track in pain. You can see this on the video footage. As you watch his face, there were tears streaming down his cheeks. Yet, in spite of his determination, it was obvious there was just no way was he going to finish; he was in too much pain.

The crowd continue to watch in amazement, some cheering, some with their hands over their mouths, as Redman was about to collapse again. Just then a man came running down out of the stands. He climbed the fence at the side of the track, got by the security guards and ran onto the track. It was his father!

He had been sitting in a section at the top of the grand stand that day; he could not imagine anything except getting involved.

For years, he had been there by his son's side, getting up at four o'clock in the morning for practices, encouraging, supporting and cheering his son on. Now, he felt he just could not stand by and let his son fail to finish the race.

So, he came jogging up to his injured son; and, when he got close enough, he reached for him, putting his hand on Derek's shoulder. Derek took a few more steps and then turned and fell into the chest of his mentor and dad. Then, Jim Redman said these words, which were later quoted in the newspaper. He said, "Derek, we started this thing together and we are going to finish this thing together."

Then, Jim took his son's arm, put it around his own shoulders, put his arm around Derek's shoulders and held his son up. I mean, literally, just held him up as together they made their way around the rest of the track. As you can imagine, the crowd was roaring its approval as Derek Redman finished his race.

But, he did not finish it alone. Together, linked arm in arm, father and son crossed the finish line as one. The crowd cheered. Who won? Don't know. Derek Redman finished with his father on his side.

Our Father runs with us too. He cheers us on with the great crowd of witnesses, letting us know we can trust Him totally. Lean on him. Oh, there will be opposition, there will be falls, challenges and disappointments but with Him by our side, we can make it. We can get to the other side.

Eyes off the storm, folks; fix your eyes on Jesus and run your race.

Chapter 9
The Questions God Asks…

What are you doing here, Elijah? — I Kings 19:9

So why would the God of the universe, the King of Kings and Lord of Lords, He who rules supremely in all matters everywhere, any time, any place, ask a puny human being a lot of questions?

I mean, think about it. He doesn't really need any answers, does He? No. The thing is, He doesn't ask questions in order to get information. So then, what's the big idea?

When God asks us a question, He's simply helping us get to where we need to get to, because it is not where we're at physically, it is where we are at spiritually that matters. Right?

The first we see of it is actually in the creation story where God is walking in the garden in the cool of the day and the Lord called to the man, "Adam, where are you?" (Genesis 3:9)

God knew exactly where Adam was, and Eve for that matter too, but the truth is they didn't. They were ashamed. They were hiding. They needed to come out of hiding and declare themselves. They needed to come before the Lord and humbly admit their mistake. God knew that, and so He asks "Adam, where are you?"

Later on in Genesis 32:27, we find that God comes down as a man (probably a pre-incarnate Jesus Christ) and wrestles with Jacob and at one point asks ol' Jake, "What is your name?"

Now why would God need to ask Jacob his name—again He knows it! So why is He asking the question? Ponder that thought.

The answer is found in the meaning of Jacob's name—schemer, deceiver, trickster. Jacob needed to declare himself before God.

He needed to humble himself, bow his head and admit "My name is…Schemer. I am a deceiver."

And it is at that point when Jacob comes out of hiding so to speak, that God declares a new identity over him.

"You shall no longer be called Jacob, but Israel because you have struggled with God and man and have overcome." (Genesis 32:28) Israel means "prince of God, or he will rule (as God) and overcomer" but again Jacob needed to declare where he was at before God changed him from the inside out. Can you imagine what it would have been like to be called a schemer all your life, then in one moment your whole life changes because you are now an overcomer? If you have ever experienced the true touch of Jesus in your life, you can no doubt relate to Jacob.

And it is interesting to see that the man formerly known as Jacob…leaves the scene with a permanent limp, just a reminder of the power of God and the weakness of man.

Think of Elijah in I Kings 18 challenging and wiping out the prophets of Baal, gaining a massive victory over the religious spirit of the day, and then later even outrunning a horse-driven chariot to a place called Jezreel. Then in only a matter of hours, he ends up running for his life and hiding in a desert, afraid of a wicked queen named Jezebel, who wants to lop his head off. Despite the huge victory that God had obtained in front of everyone, Elijah now wanders off into a month of aimlessness, winding up in a cave at Mt. Horeb where God shows up and…asks him a simple question.

"What are you doing here, Elijah?"

Once again, God gave opportunity for Elijah to speak his heart, whine about being the 'only one' left who followed God, about feeling lonely and abandoned, about all the stuff inside that had been bottled up for a season. And God meets him there and deals with his stuff before sending him on his way in a better place.

All through scripture, God asks these simple yet penetrating questions.

He asks Jeremiah, "What do you see?"

In the New Testament, you see Jesus asking questions like "Where is your husband?" to the woman at the well, whom He knows has had five husbands. He asks a beggar "Do you want to be made whole?" Well ya! Isn't it obvious? Apparently not. Apparently God needs to prompt us to declare where we are at, and what we really desire deep down before He promotes us into the next phase. He asks a blind man "What do you want from me?"

In asking a blind man that, he is asking more than whether the guy wants to see. He is asking whether the guy wants to give up his whole identity as a beggar. He is asking if he is willing to now go out and get a job, whether he is willing to return to his family and be restored into society. Everything changes when Jesus stops by! So He asks these questions to see if we realize that.

He asks the disciples "What do you want me to do for you?" He asks a crowd of hundreds who are drinking like crazy at the Feast of Tabernacles "Is anyone thirsty?"

He asks Peter "Do you love me?"

So my question for you is: what is He asking you these days?

"Where are you?"

"What is your name?

"What are you doing here?"

"What do you see?"

"What do you want me to do for you?"

"Are you thirsty? Do you love me?"

He asks you these kinds of questions, not because He doesn't know the answer but because He loves you and wants you to declare it. He wants you to humbly come before Him and tell Him your heart because He knows that when you're honest before Him, and honest with yourself, you're actually doing yourself a favor.

And He waits for you. Did you know that?

In Isaiah 30:18, we see that God is sitting and waiting for you and me to approach Him. In the Amplified Version it reads like this: "Therefore the Lord [earnestly] waits—expectant, looking and longing—to be gracious to you, and therefore He lifts Himself up that he may have mercy on you and show loving-kindness to you; for the Lord is a God of justice. Blessed—happy, fortunate [to be envied] are all those who [earnestly] wait for Him, who expect and look and long for Him, [for His victory, His favor, His love, His peace, His joy and His matchless, unbroken companionship.]"

WOW! Read that again, slowly.

What is God waiting for? We always think we are waiting for Him to act, and yet He is waiting for us! He waits for us to come to Him, to declare ourselves, to declare where we are at, to confess our sin, to give Him everything, to allow Him to change our name, our identity, from sinner to overcomer! He is waiting for us to come to Him because He longs to have compassion on us!

So another question I have for you is "Why wait any longer?"

Just put the book down, kneel if you can, but take time right now wherever you are, even if it's in a busy coffee shop, and breathe a prayer to the Lord Jesus Christ telling Him that you are thirsty for Him, that you want Him to take over the control of your life. Declare that He is Lord, and that you're sorry for trying to run the ship. Give it up. Give it all to Him and let Him lead you into the exciting life of hearing His voice every day, following after Him in every way, and bearing eternal fruit that honors His name.

It's time to be one of those polished arrows in His quiver that He takes out and uses for war! It's time to add the super to your natural and let Him live through you like never before. It's time to be a fully devoted follower of Jesus Christ! It's time to start living life from the inside out!

Chapter 10
Transition Is Forever, My Friend!

And we, who with unveiled faces, all reflect the Lord's glory, are being transformed into His likeness with ever-increasing glory, which comes from the Lord, who is Spirit — 2 Corinthians 3:18

Every time I turn around and ask someone how they are doing lately, it seems like they are saying "Well, I'm in transition, you know?"

I've realized now that no matter what anybody says, transition is forever, my friend.

We are always changing, or else we die. Medically speaking, that's true, we change or we die. We are forever growing and dying, dying and growing, both physically and spiritually.

We who are following Christ are always changing, from glory to glory, from faith to faith and from victory to victory. God wants us to change, expects us to change and enables us to change. He speaks words over our lives, then takes the time to shape us into the words He has spoken over us. It's His work. We are His workmanship, (Ephesians 2:10), His craftsmanship as He shapes us into vessels of honor to be used for His purposes for the praise of His glory (Ephesians 1:14). But if we resist changing, we will end up back in the water bucket, or slapped on the potter's wheel.

Let me explain.

In Isaiah 49:2, God uses a phrase to describe His servant Isaiah as that of "a polished arrow" hidden in his quiver. I think that we can appropriate that picture to our lives. Do you know how they made arrows back then?

Take a deep breath and read this in one breath: It was quite a process of finding the right kind of branch or stick, dropping it into a bucket of water for a time of soaking (until it was so water-logged it sunk to the bottom of the bucket), then taking it out and stretching it on a rack into a straight line, letting it dry there in the hot sun, whittling on a point to one end, sticking in some tail feathers on the other and then adjusting it to make it fly right so that it can hit the target when need be. Whew!

That is the picture of the Christian life. We are found by God under a rock somewhere, buried under the garbage and crap of life. He grabs hold of us tightly in His hand, and we are taken back to His house along with many other "sticks". We are then dropped into the water bucket of church life and we begin to soak and soak and soak, until we get kind of waterlogged. We sink. It seems we aren't really useful to anybody; we just lie there on the bottom of the bucket, watching life go by.

I heard one evangelist talking about this time in his life as being a bottom dweller in the sea of humanity. He had gotten saved and was immediately a "shark," he said, going about trying to attack everybody with the good news of the gospel. He even left tracts tucked into the toilet paper roll so it would drop out when unrolled. The fruit of his labors didn't amount to much,—and he became a bottom dweller, a guppy and just watched life go by. Then he came through a process based on the parable of the sower, realizing that his responsibility was to sow the seed in joy—like a dolphin! With a smile on his face, he just went about sowing seed and simply enjoying the good things of the kingdom. Fruit followed as He left the growing to the Grower and the sowing to the sower.

Now, back to the water bucket. After some time, the Master

Archer rescues us once again and pulls us out of the doldrums of bucket-dwelling and stretches us into upright, mature living. He then brings into focus or sharpens out the point of our life—which by the way, can be very painful—and He gives us some guidance feathers of mentors, fathers and mothers in the faith that help us fly straight. He takes us out and aims us at a target. If we miss the target on that particular outing...well it might mean going back to the water bucket! We don't fail. We just get to learn again. This is a life-long journey. But it is only after we have hit the target a few times that He tucks us away in His quiver for that special season of war.

Then there's the Potter's wheel. Remember Jeremiah 18? God instructs Jeremiah to go down to the Potter's house and listen to a message the Lord would give him. So he goes down and sees that "the pot he was shaping from the clay was marred in his hands, so the potter formed it into another pot, shaping it as it seemed best to him." (Jeremiah 18:4)

The Lord is the Master Potter and is shaping us all the time. Indeed we are marred in his hands. The original meaning of that word is 'ruined'. Well, it's a good place to be ruined—in the hands of the Master Potter. But know in the depths of your being that it is He that is shaping us, He that is molding us, and He that is making us into a vessel of honor.

The scriptures say the Potter is shaping the vessel into what seems best to him. It is so good to know that the Lord knows what He has in mind as He shapes us. We are marred in His hands. We have all sinned and fallen short of His standards, and as He shapes us, He makes us, conforms us, and forms us into what He wants us to be.

Even when Jesus said "Follow me, and I will *make* you fishers of men," the Greek word for "make" literally means to form, to construct and shape.

He shapes us. He forms us. It is His work. Sometimes it no doubt means that He splats us down on the wheel when we seem to be resisting His hand of mercy in our lives.

Another way to look at this is taken from the ever-familiar Psalm 23. This psalm is read out at so many funerals, seen in Hollywood movies so many times that we get numb to it. But the shepherd writes in Psalm 23 that the Lord "*makes* me lie down in green pastures." The word "make" there is a commanding word which literally means to put or hold down. It is a strong word. Sometimes God will *make* us lay down. You see what I mean?

Shepherds will tell of how they sometimes have to go as far as breaking the leg of a sheep that keeps wandering off, putting itself and other sheep in danger. By breaking the leg, the sheep must learn to trust the shepherd who then feeds it by hand and nurses it back to health. It is for its own good. God too is sooooooo into shaping our character into what He sees best, that He will even allow hard things to come into our life in order to shape us into the vessel of honor He desires us to be. Just ask Job, or Moses, or David, or Jesus even –who was ejected by the Spirit into the wilderness for a time of being tempted by the devil. The book of Hebrews says Jesus learned obedience by suffering—should we expect anything less in our own case?

Our character is so important because it is the vessel that holds the anointing and destiny of our lives.

Sometimes we think or pray "Oh God give me my destiny! Now!" But if He did, without having shaped our character into proper place, we could not sustain or bear up the weight of the destiny He has for us. We'd wipe out. And, then reproach is brought upon the name of Christ because of our poor witness, or hypocrisy. And He would have to judge us!

So we see that the shaping of our character is indeed forever. He is sanctifying us through and through, according to I Thessalonians 5:23 in our spirit, soul and body, keeping us "blameless" until the coming of our Lord Jesus Christ. It is a life-long process.

So I say, hang on folks. It is a ride of a lifetime, full of many short cuts and long cuts, adventures, mountains and valleys, times of great trial, wind and waves, and times of amazing green and peaceful pastures.

The key is in the submission, the "coming under the protection of" (which is what submission really means) to God and His ways, His heavenly protocol and His wisdom. He obviously allows in His wisdom what He could stop in His power—but it is always unto something. He is always training, shaping, molding, constructing us into the image of His Son whom He loves.

Don't resist His love, His discipline, His shaping. Submit to Him; submit to the process of being made into a glorious vessel of honor through which He can pour out all the goodness of His kingdom to the people around you. He wants to pour out healing oil, fine new wine; He wants to display the splendor of His fruit in you. So the bottom line is to stay the course, set your face like flint against the wind and carry on. You don't know how far you've come, and you don't know what is just the around the corner. Do everything He asks you to do, even the outrageous, illogical things that go against all human reasoning.

Kiss the bear!

Printed in the United States
47173LVS00006B/89

9 781424 124497